"Jack Dannemiller has given his life to sharing the Gospel of Jesus Christ with others. His writing is filled with solid theological background and practical helps for followers of Christ who may not have the confidence to share their hope in Jesus. My hope is that you would read this, learn from it, and go out into the world and make disciples."

—**Bill Loy,** *Served for over 40 years in Young Life of Florida, including 38 years as Area Director Lee County and Regional Training Associate.*

"Apologetics—a defense of the faith—is a neglected discipline in modern churches. Jack Dannemiller's brief introduction to the concept stresses the importance of Christians knowing what they believe and why they believe it. The key question for the claims of all religions, he points out, is, "Are they true?" Jack's journey in apologetics will demonstrate how the Christian faith is indeed true, to history and to the real world. His list of "Gems" and other resources gives readers valuable tools to strengthen their own faith, counter skeptics, and encourage seekers. I especially commend this book to parents who wish to equip their children to defend their faith as they face intellectual challenges at college and in the workplace."

—**Allen E. Hye,** *Professor Emeritus, Wright State University; Strategic Educational Consultant, College For Less, Inc.*

"When we started Agape Christian Academy 18 years ago, many still believed in absolute truth. Today there is no absolute truth, only relative truth defined by one's personal experience. We now live in a culture that has turned its back on God and His word which is leaving many in our culture without hope. A book like this will equip Christians to share the hope they have in Jesus Christ."

—**Russ and Sue Gifford,** *Founders of Agape Christian Academy*

"In *Reasons for the Faith* my friend Jack Dannemiller has provided a simple and engaging introduction to Christian apologetics. It will be an encouragement for believers in Jesus to emerge from our evangelical bubble and engage with the unbelieving world, confident that biblical Christianity really does have answers to life's great questions."

—**Dr. Andrew Hawkins,** *Serves as Senior preaching and teaching Pastor of The Village Church at Shell Point in Fort Myers, Florida. Prior to The Village Church he was Pastor of Adult Ministries at the C&MA Church in Morgantown, WV and Professor of Physical Activity and Sport Sciences at West Virginia University. He holds a Ph.D. from The Ohio State University.*

"I read this book in one morning and must say, *Reasons For The Faith* will definitely help me to better share the Gospel with anyone and everyone I encounter. Using clear, simple, intelligent language, you have written a how-to manual for sharing the Christian faith. This book will undoubtedly encourage Believers, convert unbelievers, and increase the Kingdom of Jesus Christ. Thank you and Praise God for your excellent work."

—**Michael J. Parry,** *CFRE Donor Relations Officer, The City Mission*

"Jack Dannemiller's *Reasons for the Faith* leads us through wise questions to life-giving answers. This concise book is a key to personal and cultural restoration."

—**Kelly Monroe Kullberg,** *President, Faith For Culture; Founder, the Veritas Forum; Senior Fellow, American Association of Evangelicals (AAE); Author/editor, best-selling CBA Book of the Year,* **Finding God at Harvard: Spiritual Journeys of Thinking Christians** *(Harper; IVP); Author,* **Finding God Beyond Harvard: The Quest for Veritas** *(Inter Varsity Press); Co-author, editor,* **A Faith & Culture Devotional: Daily Readings in Art, Science & Life** *(Zondervan)*

"Many people today, especially adolescents, are spiritual 'blank slates,' lacking a proper foundation on which to discern the Truth about God. I find myself often assuming that those I minister to know more about the Christian faith than they actually do, and it can be challenging to determine the necessary building blocks they might be missing in order to grow in their faith. *Reasons for the Faith* succinctly provides those key tenets of the Christian faith in a way addressing both the head and the heart. I'd encourage any new Christian or even unbelieving to utilize this book in their pursuit of grasping God's Truth."

—**Alex Meyers,** *Young Life Area Director in Cleveland, OH*

"Most books you pick up are trying to tell you what happened, tell you how you should respond, and tell you what you need. You won't find that in *Reasons For The Faith*. Instead, you will be asked significant questions, asked what you think, and asked to consider your response. What a breath of fresh air. Questions about evidence, about truth, and about faith. Jack does a wonderful job providing a clear path so that the reader's journey comes to a meaningful conclusion. Don't be afraid of good questions. They might just change your life!"

—**Don Pullen,** *Associate Pastor, The Village Church at Shell Point*

"This gem of a book is like a great full body workout. It hits on all the major areas, strengthens you, and prepares you for going out into the world."

—**Nick Dadas,** *Co-Founder of Iron Sharpens Iron – TheISILife.com*

"Having the opportunity to work with teens since 2000, I have found that one of the most important topics to continually cover with teens is apologetics. It is important for teens to know what they believe, why they believe it, and be able to know how to share what they know with their friends. This resource is an easy and quick way to teach your teens and people of all ages what to say to defend their faith and is a great resource for them to use as a guide when sharing their faith with others. Make sure to add this easy-to-use book to your toolbox when resourcing others in apologetics."

—**Pastor Kevin A. Schafer**, *Youth Pastor at Sanibel Community Church, Sanibel Island, FL*

REASONS
FOR THE
FAITH

Other Books by
JACK DANNEMILLER
from Living Dialog Ministries

Disciple Makers Toolbox
Instruction Manual: Your Guide to Becoming a Disciple Maker

Answers to YOUR Greatest Questions
A Journey in Discovering God's Wisdom

Your Invitation
Small group exploration of the Gospel according to Mark

Transformation
Small group exploration of the Gospel according to John

Lighting the Way
Small group exploration of Paul's Letter to the Romans

Renewing Your Mind - Thinking as a Christian
Small group exploration of a Christian Worldview

JACK DANNEMILLER

REASONS FOR THE FAITH

A JOURNEY IN CHRISTIAN APOLOGETICS

Living Dialog™ | Be a new creation
MINISTRIES

Living Dialog™ MINISTRIES | Be a new creation

Reasons for the Faith
© 2023 The Living Dialog Ministries (TLDM)
Published by The Living Dialog Ministries, Richmond, VA
www.livingdialog.org

ISBN: 979-8-9863804-3-8

TLDM, Inc. is a tax-exempt organization under section 501(c) (3) of the Internal Revenue Code effective 2 December 2009. We do our work and fulfill our mission through the generous gifts of our friends around the world. Your tax-deductible gifts may be sent to TLDM — PO Box 15125 — Richmond, VA 23227

10 9 8 7 6 5 4 3 2 1

Printed in the United States of America

Cover Design: Marlene Asta

TABLE OF CONTENTS

This book is dedicated to all the faithful followers of Jesus Christ that want to be sure of What they Believe, Why they Believe It and Why Christianity is True.

REASONS FOR THE FAITH

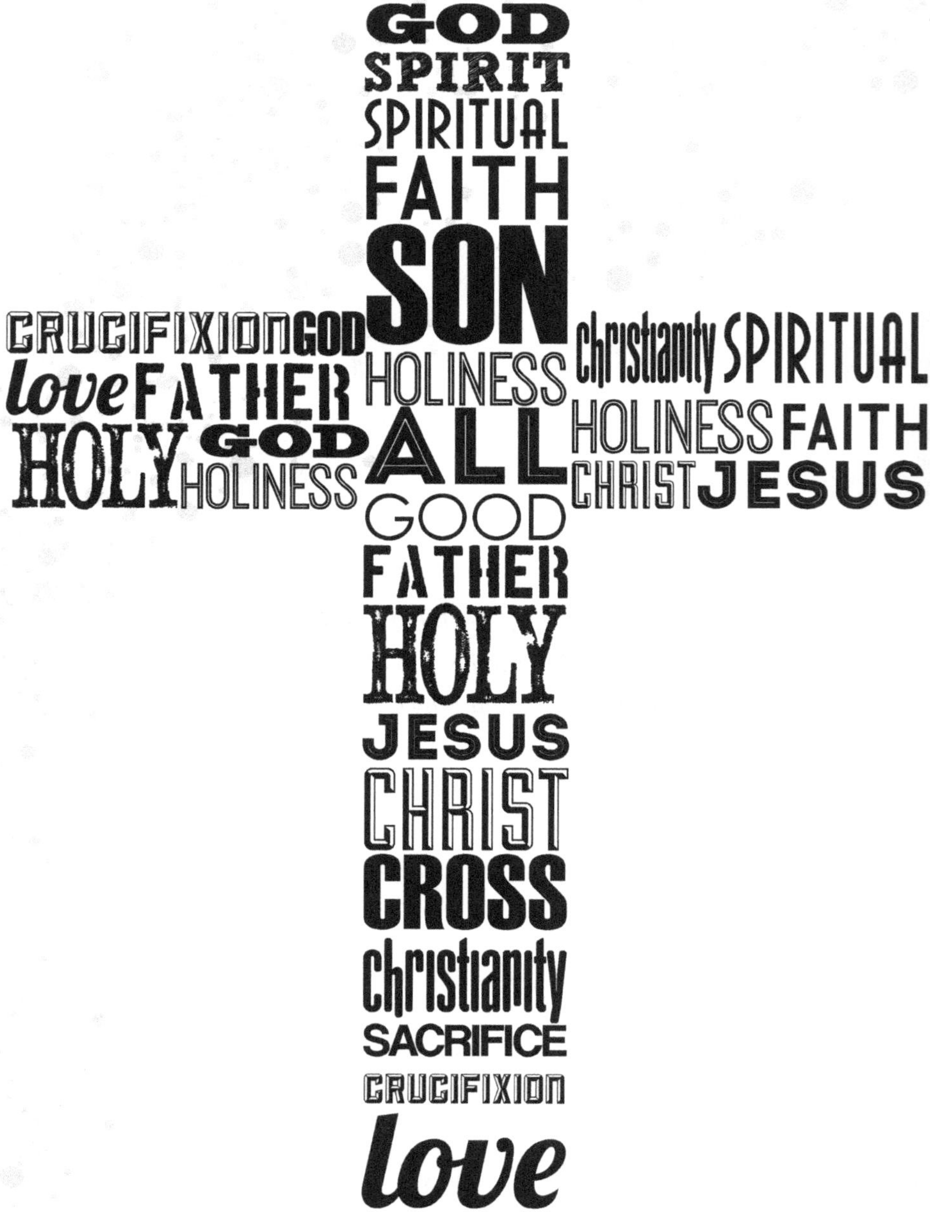

FOREWORD

Against all odds, headline news stories this year include two "revivals." One such outpouring arose at Asbury University, in Kentucky, still touching lives around the world. The other revival, of the 1960s, is rendered in the film Jesus Revolution, shocking Hollywood by its expanding audience and rave reviews.

At the same time, like lethal drugs, cynicism and enmity are also pervasive. When biblical faith and culture fade, the human person is demoralized, and power becomes "truth."

Despite the unrelenting campaigns of social engineers to demoralize, isolate, divide, indoctrinate, dull and dumb us into submission, revival, in our "post-Christian" and "post-truth" century, still happens. God is restoring all things. The hunger for truth and for God seems built into the human soul.

Seekers and believers want Truth, but how do we know anything to be certain and true? Revival best leads to the transformation of our minds – and culture. Emotions and experiences are gifts, but the heart cannot long follow what the mind does not firmly believe.

In *Reasons for the Faith*, Jack Dannemiller clears the fog and gives us bright, precise definitions of and reasons for, the Christian faith:

- What Christians believe, and why we believe it.
- Why follow Jesus, and why he matters.
- The uniqueness of Christianity in contrast to other religions.
- Why be equipped to share the gospel.

Mr. Dannemiller shows us how to think, believe and therefore walk in courageous faith—just as Paul the Apostle urged us to "give a reason for the hope within you... with gentleness and respect." (I Peter 3:15). Why? For the sake of a hurting world that God so loves.

Thousands of people, young and old, are coming home to the truth of God and His love for us. They join billions of believers throughout history. This takes forms of repentance for sin, worship and gratitude for God's grace, and we hope the long-term fruit of discipleship and mission.

Biblical truth yields personal and cultural restoration and reformation - what we call advancing God's kingdom for His glory, and human flourishing, as we apply truth in every sphere of life and culture: Personal character, the family, work and economics, engineering, education, law and government, the arts and sciences, hospitality and healthcare. All of life is meaningful, because of God's love in Jesus.

What a joy to play even a small part in the advancement of God's kingdom, "on Earth as in Heaven." This small but mighty book is a key to our best life, culture and future.

Because of love,

Kelly M. Kullberg (Kelly Monroe Kullberg)
President, Faith For Culture; Founder, the Veritas Forum
Senior Fellow, American Association of Evangelicals (AAE);
Author/editor, best-selling CBA Book of the Year, *Finding God at Harvard: Spiritual Journeys of Thinking Christians* (Harper; IVP); Author, *Finding God Beyond Harvard: The Quest for Veritas* (Inter Varsity Press); Co-author, editor, *A Faith & Culture Devotional: Daily Readings in Art, Science & Life* (Zondervan)

ACKNOWLEDGMENTS

I am especially grateful for the support and encouragement of family, friends, colleagues, and Brothers-in-Christ in creating books for Christian discipleship. I am thankful for my long-time friend, Reverend Irving Stubbs, for introducing me to the disciplines of dialogue and for being the co-author of our *Living Dialogue Collection* of discipleship studies. The entire leadership team at TLDM has been so faithful in backing the publication of all the writings including this project.

I want to acknowledge the many contributions to the topic of apologetics by the men's Discovery group at Sanibel Community Church and for our dialogues on the practice of thinking as a Christian. I would be remiss if I failed to mention the many pastors and Bible teachers who have poured their love and scriptural truths into my life these past 80+ years. Also, I have been blessed by the ideas and writings of so many other Christian authors that have contributed to my knowledge of Christian apologetics.

I am indebted to Brian Regrut, Executive director of The Living Dialog Industries (TLDM), for his excellent editing and ideas for the layout of the book. In the same light, our marketing partner, Paradise Creative Group, including: Katrina Salokar, Marlene Asta, Jennifer Scott, Ava St. Laurent, Frank Gutboard, and the others on their team who have made many great suggestions on how to "make it better." They also created an eye-catching cover for the book.

Finally, I am eternally grateful for the inspiration of the Holy Spirit who guided me to the Biblical Truths contained in this book so that it would be life-transforming to its readers, Christians, and seekers alike and bring Glory to God and Jesus my Savior.

INTRODUCTION

Many religions make claims that they know the way to God and an eternal destiny in Paradise/Heaven. The question is, are they true? Is there one religion or faith that has reasons that sync with reality and evidence to back up its claims? Is there absolute Truth that exists which can be discovered to convince a person beyond any reasonable doubt? If these questions resonate with you and your sense of curiosity, then this is just the book you will certainly want to explore. It will take you on a journey of discovery that will change your life forever. It will give you the confidence to live every day to the fullest, have peace within your soul and with God and you will know for certain about your eternal destiny. Guaranteed!

THIS BOOK IS DESIGNED TO GIVE YOU A CLEAR AND COMPREHENSIVE, BUT NON-EXHAUSTIVE INTRODUCTION TO THE WORLD OF APOLOGETICS.

The title of the book has been chosen to appeal to a rational mind and a gentle and humble heart. Mankind has been created in the image of God with the ability to reason. This gift of reason differentiates man from all the other creatures in nature. Being created in the image of God, who is eternal, affirms that we as humans are also eternal. In other words, we are both physical and spiritual. To put it in clear terms, we are spiritual beings with heart, soul, mind and conscience having a physical experience. So, when the physical experience ends what happens to the soul, the eternal you? That is the profound question and one of many other similar great questions that are answered in this book on apologetics.

The term apologetics, as used in this book, will focus specifically on Christian apologetics. Apologetics does not mean apologizing! The definition that is provided in this book may surprise you if you are unfamiliar with the term. You will not be in the minority but rather in the majority that has never considered the idea or topic of apologetics. There have been many books and studies on this topic. This book is designed to give you a clear and comprehensive, but non-exhaustive, introduction to the world of apologetics. So, we invite you to fasten your seatbelt and get ready for a fast and exciting journey into the world of Christian apologetics, the Reasons for The Faith. Enjoy!

For God so loved.
the world that
He gave his one
and only Son, that
whoever believes
in him shall not
perish but have
eternal life.

CHAPTER 1

DEFINITION OF CHRISTIAN APOLOGETICS

The word apologetics is somewhat misleading and has nothing to do with apologizing in the modern sense of the word. The common definition of apologetics is reasoned arguments in justification of someone or a cause. Persuading with reason, evidence and truth. Christian apologetics means making a reasonable case for the following:

- The existence of God.
- The intelligent design of Creation including all nature and the cosmos.
- Jesus Christ, the promised Messiah, the Son of God, and the only way to Heaven and eternal life.
- That there will be a judgment day of God.
- That Jesus is coming back as King of Kings and Lord of Lords.
- The Bible is the inspired Word of God.
- That God is the source of objective morality.
- That Truth exists and anything that contradicts it is false.
- That God has a plan of redemption for sinful mankind.
- That Bible prophecies are 100% true and accurate.
- That Heaven and Hell are real places.

In Christian Biblical terms, a concise definition of apologetics is **What Christians believe, Why they believe it and Why it is important.** Many more details about Christian apologetics will be given in the chapters that follow. You might be wondering, "why is it important to have an understanding of apologetics in our culture today?" That is a very valid question that will be addressed in the next chapter. The answer is especially important for all Christians who want to be able to effectively contend for and defend the Christian faith. This knowledge will prepare you to be able to share the gospel with confidence.

CHAPTER 2
WHY IS IT IMPORTANT TO UNDERSTAND APOLOGETICS?

Why is it important for Christians to know about and understand apologetics? The single most important answer to this question is so that they will be able to share their testimony and the gospel message based on the Truth of the Christian faith. The Bible is God's instruction manual for life. God has provided guidelines and commandments for living a meaningful and purpose-driven life that honors and brings glory to God. As Christians, we are given the privilege of being a partner with God and with Jesus to build his kingdom. What follows is a list of reasons why Christians need to understand apologetics and use them for God's intended purpose.

HERE ARE THE REASONS:

- First, God's desire is that no one is condemned or lost *[John 3:16]*. Christians' role in this partnership is to be Christ's ambassadors sharing God's love as we are going in life so that others will know Jesus as Savior and Lord *[Luke 10:27]*.

- For believers to be able to both contend for and defend the Christian faith with boldness and confidence and never be ashamed to be a follower of Jesus *[Romans 1:16]*.

- To be able to share the faith message based on documented facts and evidence. To know Biblical truth, especially the evidence of Jesus' death on the cross and His resurrection. These two events are the foundation of the Christian faith *[John 14:6]*.

- To lovingly obey Jesus' command to fulfill the great commission as you are going in life *[Matthew 28:19, Luke 9:26, Mark 8:38]*. Jesus said, "If you love me, obey my commandments." *[John 14:15]*.

- Many millennials and their children are not responding to the Gospel. They are not attending church or even sending their children either. They need to learn the truth from friends who care. Faith comes by hearing the good news of God's love and forgiveness of sin. [**NOTE**: See the poem, *My Friend*, in the Appendix on page 45.]

- Equally troubling is that 70% of youth from Christian homes and even those who attended church youth groups are leaving the faith. The Church and their parents and grandparents need to be able to answer their questions to overcome their unbelief. How bad is it? A recent Barna Survey indicated that only 2% of generation Z youth, 16-year-olds, have a biblical worldview. This generation has been "brainwashed" by the schools that teach Evolution as if it were true even though there is no evidence to supportthe theory. Evolution is actually a religion - no god - masquerading as a science - no evidence.

What unbelief you might ask? The following is a list of the truths that are not accepted by Generation Z. In other words, they do not believe:

1. That the God of Creation and of the Bible exists.
2. That the Bible is God's living Word and contains Truth.
3. That Jesus is the only Savior and way to peace with God and eternal life.

4. That Jesus is coming again.
5. That Heaven and Hell are real places and the only destinations for human souls.
6. That God knows the future, as He exists outside of time and space.
7. That God actually sees human history as complete.

NOTE: A recent Pew survey of Americans' religious beliefs indicated that 93% believe that when they die they're going to Heaven. However, the truth is that Heaven is not the default location for the unsaved. Hell is! The fact is that God sends no one to Hell. People use their free will to choose to go there when they reject God's gift of grace and forgiveness in Jesus. It is not for lack of evidence that people reject God's offer of salvation but rather because they have hardened hearts to the Truth of God's word and choose to go their own way.

Finally, it is important to understand Christian apologetics so that Christian believers are equipped with a thorough understanding of what they believe and why they believe it and will be able to contend for and defend, when necessary, their Christian faith in the current secular humanistic culture. We all want to be able to stand strong in the face of challenge and persecution so that one day when we are face-to-face with Jesus we will hear these words, "Well done good and faithful servant. Enter into the joy of the Lord prepared for you before the foundation of the world." *[Matthew 25:34]* AMEN!!

CHAPTER 3
WHAT CHRISTIANS BELIEVE

Throughout the ages, people have tried to understand basic ideas that are contained in the Bible so that they can more easily understand God and live out their daily lives with meaning and purpose. This kind of thinking is called theology. This term comes from the Greek meaning the study of the nature of God. Christian theology defines what Christians believe. This theology has two foundational beliefs: (1) special revelation, the Bible, and (2) general revelation, the evidence of Intelligent Design in the Creation. Christians believe that all history, philosophy, science, mathematics, reasoning, and all life experiences confirm the existence of God as the creator, redeemer, and sole provider of human salvation from sin and forgiveness through faith in Jesus Christ.

This undertaking, the writing of this book, is an attempt to understand the sources of Christian belief in the Bible, in Christian worship, and in Creeds and Confessions that have been developed by Christians over the past 2,000 years. As we continue to present what Christians believe, it is important to remember that the human mind is not capable of adequately or fully understanding or describing God. That's a good thing. Who wants a god who is no bigger than a human mind? However, God gave us brains and a mind so that we can learn and remember. He provided an invitation to come and "Reason Together"*[Isaiah 1:18]*. Therefore, you do not have to 'check your brains at the door' to be a believing Christian, thank God!

SO, WHAT DO CHRISTIANS BELIEVE?

First, they believe in the existence of God. Christians believe that God is Holy, Eternal, and Relational, and has a personality characterized by Love. That He has a master plan which covers the entire span of human history from Creation through redemption, salvation, judgment, and eternity. That salvation is by God's Grace alone, through Faith alone, in Jesus Christ alone *[Ephesians 2:8]*!

What is believed includes knowledge, not opinions, about Creation versus Evolution, nature, the origins of man created in God's image, that sin is real, that objective morality exists and that stewardship of man's time, talents, and treasures and the planet's resources are to be used wisely and responsibly to build God's kingdom and provide for the needs of human life. That God created family and marriage between a man and a woman as the foundation for a safe, just, and moral society.

Further, Christians believe that Heaven and Hell are real places and that the Christian church was established to proclaim the "Good News" of the gospel of Jesus Christ to the entire world. They also believe that the Bible is God's inspired Word and therefore is Truth *[2 Timothy 3:16]*. They believe that there will be a judgment day for all those who have rejected God's offer of grace and salvation in Jesus. That one day Jesus is coming back to take his rightful role as King of Kings and Lord of Lords over all of Creation. They also believe that God is going to create a New Heaven and New Earth as the dwelling place for all true believers and their 'saved' loved ones. That He will be present with them along with the heavenly host, and the saints of the ages for all eternity *[Revelation 21:1]*.

Finally, Christians believe that the Bible is God's instruction manual for life. That the Bible contains Truth, Wisdom, and the instructions every person needs to live life as God designed it. God has provided principles and Ten Commandments on how to live in peace and harmony with Him and with others. It has been often said that the word Bible is also an acronym, meaning, Best Investigated Before Leaving Earth. That is one reason that it is still the most published and treasured of all books. In reality, a person will never be truly wise or have discernment if he or she has never diligently studied the Bible. The wisdom of man is foolishness to God *[1 Corinthians 3:19]*.

A concise statement of what Christians believe is in the Apostles' Creed which follows in the next section. After reading it, you will then journey on to the explanation of, 'Why they Believe.' You will find the reasons and evidence truly amazing.

Faith
Love
Grace
Hope
HOPE
LOVE Mercy LOVE
Faith
Faith Hope
Grace

CHAPTER 4
THE APOSTLES' CREED

The Apostles' Creed is a good starting point as a summary of what Christians believe. It is well worth remembering and memorizing. In some ways, it's much like our Pledge of Allegiance to the flag. It is a concise statement of the Christian's allegiance to God.

I believe in God,
The Father Almighty,
Creator of Heaven and Earth.

I believe in Jesus Christ, His only Son, our Lord,
Who was conceived by the Holy Spirit
And born of the Virgin Mary,
He suffered under Pontius Pilate,
Was crucified, died and was buried;
He descended to Hell.
The third day he rose again from the dead;
He ascended into Heaven
And sitteth at the right hand of God,
the Father Almighty,
From thence He will come
To judge the living and the dead.

I believe in the Holy Spirit,
The Holy Christian Church,
The Communion of Saints,
The Forgiveness of Sins,
The Resurrection of the Body,
And the Life Everlasting.

Amen.

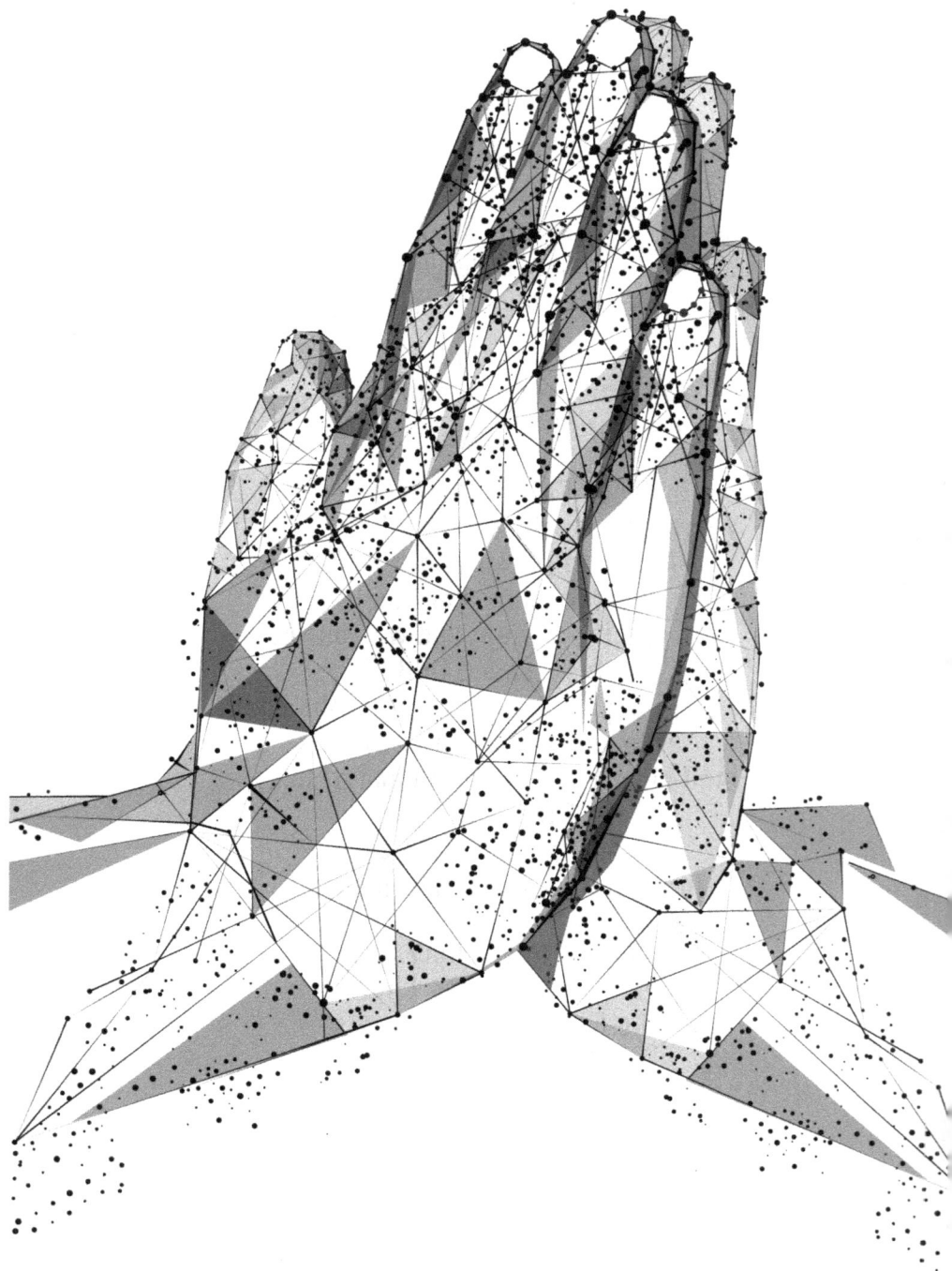

CHAPTER 5
WHY CHRISTIANS BELIEVE IT

The second part of Christian apologetics will be explored in this segment of the book. We will now focus on 'Why Christians Believe It' and put their faith in God and Jesus Christ. Christian believers start with the concept that the Bible is the inspired Word of God and therefore totally reliable as the truth about what it contains. Christians believe the truth exists and can be discovered and anything that contradicts it is false. In fact, that is actually known as the Law of Non-Contradiction. They trust the evidence that proves the Bible is historically correct, that it is the best documented of all ancient books and contains prophecy that is 100% accurate. They believe this is true because God can see the future of human history as if it is already completed.

To confirm why Christians believe that God knows the future and that prophecy comes from Him, we will look at two examples out of thousands. In 700 BC, the prophet, Micah, prophesied that the Messiah, Yeshua (Jesus), would be born in Bethlehem Ephrathah in Israel. That is exactly what happened. This prophecy is just one of 100 about the 1st and 2nd coming of Jesus. By the way, there were two Bethlehems in Israel at that time. Bethlehem Ephrathah was the smaller town and birthplace of King David. The prophecy was very specific as to location to avoid any confusion. [**NOTE:** For more prophecies about Jesus, see the list in the appendix.]

The second prophecy was given by two prophets, Isaiah and Ezekiel. In the book of *Isaiah chapter 23* and *Ezekiel chapter 26*, there is a message from God about the future judgment of the very wealthy but idol-worshiping cities of Tyre on the East coast of the Mediterranean. The Prophets pronounced that the cities would be totally destroyed, never to be rebuilt, and would only be a place for fishermen to dry their nets. In 580 BC, Nebuchadnezzar attacked the land fortress of Tyre. The siege of the city lasted 15 years. Nebuchadnezzar, having exhausted his materiel and army, left and never conquered the sea fortress of Tyre. But God's words are truth and here is what happens next. In 332 BC, Alexander the Great decided to attack the island fortress of Tyre. What he did was use the rubble left by Nebuchadnezzar to build a causeway from the land to the island where he successfully plundered and destroyed the city. The only activity at Tyre today is fishermen drying their nets just as was prophesied. These examples and hundreds of others like them are why Christians have Faith in God's Word.

Further, Christians know that the Bible is a miracle in its own right, as it was written over a period of 1,500 years by 40 authors in complete harmony without any contradictions in its 66 books. Christian believers trust and accept the evidence of both the secular, Josephus [AD 38-97] and Tacitus [AD 56-113] and biblical records of the life teachings, miracles, death by crucifixion, resurrection [500 witnesses], and the ascension to Heaven of Jesus Christ where He resides today at the right hand of God as the Intercessor for Christian's prayers. [**NOTE:** If you want a pre-incarnation look at Jesus on His throne, check out *Isaiah 6:1-3*. To see Jesus in His resurrected glory, check out *Revelation 1:13-16*]

If these reasons were not enough, Christians believe the evidence and testimonies of the dramatically transformed lives of Jesus' 11 closest disciples who were all martyred, except for John, for proclaiming the truth of the gospel message, "Jesus; crucified, buried, and resurrected, the promised Messiah." They all saw the risen Savior in person and were committed to telling the world the 'Good News.' The fact is that no one ever willingly dies or is martyred for a lie! The disciples were all willing to die for the Truth. Additionally, we have all seen the miraculous contributions of Christianity to Western Civilization in the areas of literature, art, science, music, mathematics, medicine, education, philosophy, law and so much more.

Finally, there are the witness and testimonies of the hundreds of millions of followers of Jesus Christ through the centuries. Why so many believers? The answer is, they believed God's Word and that Jesus is the only way to eternal life and a transformed life full of meaning and purpose. He is 'The Way' to receive God's gifts of joy, love, peace, forgiveness, contentment, and eternal life. Jesus is the only way to receive God's gift of Grace *[Ephesians 2:8 & John 14:6]*.

So many reasons, so many believers, so much truth, and so much evidence, make one wonder why everyone isn't a Christian. The answer seems to be because so many people want to live by their own rules, not God's, have their own truth, not the Bible's, be guided by their own subjective moral beliefs, not God's objective morality and in effect be their own God. In their pride, they refuse to humble themselves and put God on the "throne" of their lives. These choices reflect the condition of a 'hard heart', one not willing to receive God's gifts of Grace and Forgiveness in Jesus. If they don't humble themselves and repent, one day they will face God's judgment.

CHAPTER 6
WHY BE A FOLLOWER OF JESUS?

This list is included here as it is one way to present the value of becoming a believer and a disciple-maker. It points out the many benefits of following Jesus. He offers everyone who trusts in him the certainty of a life-transforming, personal and intimate relationship. It is the 'Good News' of the best way to live and the only way to die. A relationship with Jesus brings peace with God. He alone is the answer to personal contentment in a world and culture overflowing with chaos and evil. So, why follow Jesus? The answer is because He is who He said He is. HE is:

- The Son of God
- The Christ and Redeemer
- The prophesied Messiah
- Emmanuel, "God with us"
- The only Way to Heaven and eternal life
- The only Way to peace with God
- The only One to forgive sin
- The only Hope for the world
- The Light of the world
- The 'Lamb of God' who takes away the sins of the world
- The Good Shepherd who looks after His sheep
- The Promise Giver and Promise Keeper
- The Word of Life
- The only Intercessor between man and God

- The source of Wisdom, Grace and Love
- The One who gives meaning and purpose to life
- The Great Physician and Healer
- The Jesus who is coming back to judge the world
- The King of Kings and Lord of Lords
- The One who will reign forever with the saints/believers

AND MUCH MORE!!! ALLELUIA and AMEN!!!

CHAPTER 7

WHY BE EQUIPPED TO SHARE THE GOSPEL?

In this section, we will briefly explore the question, Why be equipped to share the gospel? We will offer some suggestions on how to engage in dialogue with others and also look at some ideas on how to be more effective in leading seekers into a personal relationship with Jesus Christ. You will also be alerted to some of the questions that usually arise when sharing the gospel message along with appropriate answers. Lastly, you will be offered some resources that are available from our ministry's website, LivingDialog.org, that will aid you in presenting the message and your testimony.

The answer to the question is quite simple. Jesus has required all believers to be about fulfilling the "Great Commission" *[Mark 16:15]* as they are going in life. This is not a suggestion. It is a command from the Savior. It is with hearts filled with gratitude and humility for all He has given us that every believer should joyfully obey. Jesus said, "If you love me, keep my commandments." *[John 14:15]*. Believers should all be like the Apostle Paul as he stated in *Romans 1:16*, "I am not ashamed of the gospel of Christ, because it is the power of God that brings salvation to everyone who believes."

Now let's consider the topic of dialogue. You might wonder, "What is Dialogue?" Dialogue is the ancient art of seeking Truth by engaging others in searching for answers to the profound questions of life. Why am I here? What is my purpose? Does God Exist? Is there life beyond death? What happens when I die? What do Christians believe? How is Christianity unique versus other religions? And many more. In sharing the gospel, believers need to be equipped to answer these and other questions. Employing dialogue methods is the best way to keep others engaged in the conversation.

The first principle of Christian dialogue is to answer questions and ask your questions with love and grace. It is true that people don't care how much you know until they know how much you care. Questions in this section are designed to draw out other personal beliefs and perspectives and engage them in the discussion that leads to sharing Biblical truths and the gospel. In dialogue, the best practice is to be open-minded as you and the other person inquire, explore, discover and seek an understanding of God's Word, the Bible. The goal is for the other party to get their questions answered, their curiosity satisfied, and finally decide to follow Jesus.

Each encounter presents different challenges, so disciples need to have flexibility on how to direct dialogue. When the Holy Spirit leads your conversation to spiritual matters you might say, "Tell me about your spiritual journey." Or, "When you think about Christianity, what comes to mind? " Or, "What do you think happens when you die?" Or perhaps, "So how are you with Jesus?" This is a slight rephrasing of the question, "Who is Jesus to you?" Any of these questions can open up a special opportunity to share the gospel message, your story, and the love of God with someone who is genuinely seeking answers to some of life's most searching questions. Depending on their responses, you could follow up with one or more of the questions from the list below.

HERE ARE THE QUESTIONS:

- That's curious. Where did you get that idea?
- Are there facts that support your view?
- How do you know those facts are true? What is the evidence?
- What makes you think that's a good idea?
- Can you tell me more about that?
- I am not sure I understand what you said. Would you please repeat it?
- That is interesting. Would you tell me more about it?
- If what you believe was not true, would you want to know?

At some point in the conversation, a good question would be, "Would you like to know Jesus?" They may be ready to invite Jesus into their life as Lord and Savior. All that's left to do then is to lead them in a prayer to accept Christ and begin their faith journey. Remember we do not save anyone. Salvation is the act of the Holy Spirit. Believers are just the bearers of the "Good News."

Finally, there are a few Bible verses you should have written down or put on your phone or memorized to show someone what God has to say about their need for Jesus. They are called, "The Pathway to Heaven and Eternal Life." The verses are:

- "For all have sinned and fall short of the glory of God," *[Romans 3:23]*
- "But God demonstrates his own love for us in this: While we were still sinners, Christ died for us." *[Romans 5:8]*
- "For the wages of sin is death, but the gift of God is eternal life in Christ Jesus our Lord." *[Romans 6:23]*

- "For God so loved the world that he gave his one and only Son, that whoever believes in him shall not perish but have eternal life." *[John 3:16]*

- "And this is the testimony: God has given us eternal life, and this life is in His Son. Whoever has the Son has life; whoever does not have the Son of God does not have life." *[1 John 5:11-12]*

- "If you declare with your mouth, "Jesus is Lord," and believe in your heart that God raised Him from the dead, you will be saved." *[Romans 10:9]*

It is best when you share these and have the other person read them aloud. Why? Because Faith comes by hearing, hearing the Word of God! *[Romans 10:17]*

NOTE: A handout of A *Pathway To Heaven* is available as are other "Helps" including the booklets, "A*nswers to Life's Greatest Questions*" and "*Light of The World - What Happens When I Die*" and study guides for evangelism outreach and Discipleship from the Living Dialog Ministries website, LivingDialog.org. They can be seen on the pages after the Appendix.

CHAPTER 8

CHRISTIANITY VS OTHER RELIGIONS

What makes Christianity unique when compared to the other world religions? This is a frequent topic of conversation among Christians, those who are of different religions and those seeking answers to life's basic questions about God and eternity. Many believe, although not true, that all religions offer a path to God and being created in the 'image of God' makes everyone a 'child of God.'

The seven paragraphs that follow provide a robust and comprehensive perspective on the subject. We believe these paragraphs bring consistent clarity to this topic.

HERE ARE THE 7 RESPONSES FROM THE SURVEY:

1. The simple answer is, Jesus! Why? Because He alone saves *[John 14:6]*. Christianity is the one and only faith that promises assurance of the forgiveness of sins, peace with God, and eternal life. Jesus' sinless life, teachings, miracles, death on the cross, resurrection, and ascension into Heaven is the foundation upon which the Christian faith is based. That is the Good News! Christianity is unique among all other religions in that it is based not on what a person does to gain favor with God, good works, but on what God has done to restore a broken relationship between man and God. It is known as God's Amazing Grace.

2. Jesus is the answer because salvation is by God's grace alone, through faith alone, in Jesus Christ alone. Only Christianity offers the absolute assurance of eternal life as it is a gift of God's Grace for all who by faith repent of their sins and trust in Jesus as Savior and Lord *[Ephesians 2:8]*. Christianity is about Jesus, the cross (forgiveness of sins), His resurrection, and His second coming. The founders of all other religions are dead. They offered some sound platitudes for living a moral life, but no hope for eternity based on solid evidence. They are religions of good works and self-sacrifice to get a pardon for the worshiper's sins. Christianity is unique in that only by faith in Jesus are sins forgiven.

3. The person of Jesus Christ and the Holy Bible differentiate Christianity. The cross of Christ forever bridged the gap between sinners and a Holy God. The Bible, rightly called the book that made our world, has inspired the best of Western civilization: science, technology, education, and political and economic freedom. Because we are made in God's image, Christianity values human dignity and liberates those who are often marginalized in other cultures: slaves, women, children, and outcasts.

4. Christianity's primary doctrine is that all of the worshiper's sins and wrongdoings, including that past, present, and future have been paid for by God Himself and such a pardon is a gift from God accepted once by faith in His son Jesus who paid the penalty for such sins by His death on the cross.

Whereas, all other religions require good works and religious activity of the worshipers to get a pardon for the worshiper's sins. In Christianity, we are saved by God's grace not by our good works.

5. Christianity is unique in that it expresses and believes there is, inside the Godhead, an all-embracing, self-giving, dynamic love between Father, Son, and Holy Spirit, so it can be truly said, "God is Love". Mankind feels the need for power beyond itself but often defines that from man's finitude. Mankind makes images, fashions theologies to negotiate and 'cut' deals with God developing rituals that often misrepresent God. Christianity represents God as all-powerful, all-knowing, present everywhere, whose Nature is Love, who redeems and empowers those who accept and trust God's Grace (i.e., salvation in Jesus Christ).

6. Christian faith, is not man-made, but God-revealed! Therefore universal validity is based on the conviction of the deity, authority, and exclusive claims of the historic Christ as revealed in the Bible. Christ was (and is) Himself the message. The answer to the fundamental questions of all religions is, "Can I know God? What is He like?". The answer has been given in the life, death, and resurrection of the Lord Jesus Christ, for He alone removed the barrier of sin which separates man from God. It is just here, that Christianity is unique. All other religions teach what man must do, where as Christianity alone tells what God has already done in Christ.

7. Two phrases differentiate Christianity from all other world religions; 'in order that' and 'because of.' 'In order that' you can gain favor with God, you must keep ALL the rituals and make ALL the sacrifices. The reality is that in other religions you never know if or when you have done enough. Whereas, with Christianity, 'because of' Jesus Christ *[Ephesians 2:8]* you can have a relationship and peace with God, have your sins forgiven, receive the gift of eternal life and have the absolute certainty of Heaven *[John 14:6 & 1 John 5:12]*. World religions are man-made. Christianity is God Inspired!

The common theme through the seven perspectives, which were provided by distinguished Church pastors, Bible teachers, and Christian Authors, is Jesus Christ the resurrected Savior. He is the only way to peace with God, eternal life and Heaven. They also underscore the Sovereignty of God, the Truth of the Bible and God's plan of Redemption for sinners, the Cross of Christ.

CHAPTER 9
GEMS OF WISDOM
MESSIANIC PROPHECIES AND FULFILLMENT

For the Gospel writers, one of the main reasons for believing in Jesus was the way His life fulfilled the Old Testament prophecies about the Messiah. Following is a list of some of the main prophecies.

PROPHECY	OLD TESTAMENT PROPHECY	NEW TESTAMENT FULFILLMENT
Messiah was to be born in Bethlehem	Micah 5:2	Matthew 2:1-6 Luke 2:1-20
Messiah was to be born of a virgin	Isaiah 7:14	Matthew 1:18-25 Luke 1:26-38
Messiah was to be a prophet like Moses	Deuteronomy 18:15, 18, 19	John 7:40
Messiah was to enter Jerusalem in triumph	Zachariah 9:9	Matthew 21:1-9 John 12:12-16
Messiah was to be rejected by His own people	Isaiah 53:1, 3 Psalm 118:22	Matthew 26:3, 4 John 12:37-43 Acts 4:1-12
Messiah was to be betrayed by one of His followers	Psalm 41:19	Matthew 26:14-16, 47-50 Luke 22:19-23
Messiah was to be tried and condemned	Isaiah 53:8	Luke 23:1-25 Matthew 27:1, 2
Messiah was to be silent before His accusers	Isaiah 53:7	Matthew 27:12-14 Mark 15:3-4 Luke 23:8-10

PROPHECY	OLD TESTAMENT PROPHECY	NEW TESTAMENT FULFILLMENT
Messiah was to be struck and spat upon by his enemies	Isaiah 50:6	Matthew 26:67, 27:30 Mark 14:65
Messiah was to be mocked and taunted	Psalm 22:7,8	Matthew 27:39-44 Luke 23:11, 35
Messiah was to die by crucifixion	Psalm 22:14, 16, 17	Matthew 27:31 Mark 15:20, 25
Messiah was to suffer with criminals and pray for his enemies	Isaiah 53:12	Matthew 27:38 Mark 15:27, 28 Luke 23:32-34
Messiah was to be given vinegar and gall	Psalm 69:21	Matthew 27:34 John 19:28-30
Others were to cast lots for Messiah's garments	Psalm 22:18	Matthew 27:35 John 19:23, 24
Messiah's bones were not to be broken	Exodus 12:46	John 19:31-36
Messiah was to die as a sacrifice for sin	Isaiah 53:5, 6, 8, 10, 11, 12	John 1:29; 11:49-52 Acts 10:43; 13:38, 39
Messiah was to be raised from the dead	Psalm 16:10	Acts 2:22-32 Matthew 28:1-10
Messiah is now at God's right hand	Psalm 110:1	Mark 16:19 Luke 24:50, 51

Source: *Prophecies of Jesus Fulfilled by Mary Fairchild, learnreligions.com*

WHAT DOES GOD WANT FOR HIS CHILDREN?

* **TRUST**: In Him as Creator and Father of the Lord Jesus Christ *[Genesis 1:1]*.

* **BELIEVE**: In Jesus as Lord and Savior *[John 1:1-5, 1 John 5:12]*.

* **LOVE**: God and your neighbor as yourself *[Luke 10:27]*.

* **TRUTH**: Know God's living Word, The Bible, and live it! Memorize it *[John 14:6, John 8:32]*.

* **SHARE**: The Gospel—The Great Commission, as you are going about life each day *[Matthew 28:19]*.

* **OBEY**: His Ten Commandments *[Exodus 20]*.

* **GRACE**: Receive His salvation and blessings with gratitude *[Ephesians 2:8]*.

* **MERCY**: Extend grace and mercy to others as God has shown His to you.

* **PURIFICATION**: Daily seek to remove from your life those thoughts, comments and habits that prevent you from becoming more like Jesus. Be made Righteous and Holy *[1 John 1:9]*.

* **SANCTIFICATION**: Become more like Jesus every day in every way *[Ephesians 1:4-6]*.

* **QUIET TIME**: Set aside time for a daily experience with God to fully and intimately know Him. A time of prayer and reflection will help you discern God's will, His good, pleasing and perfect will for your life *[Romans 12:2]*. Have time to let go and let God rule and reign in your life. A time to enjoy just being in God's presence, to experience fully His unfailing love, to be immersed in His Amazing Grace, to reflect on

His promises, to be renewed by the Holy Spirit, to receive His 'marching orders' for the day and to commit to live life to honor Him in everything.

- **WORSHIP**: Regularly participate in worship services in a Christ-centered, gospel-preaching church. Join a small group Bible study. Attend a disciple-making Sunday school class. Become equipped to contend for and defend the reasons for your faith. Discover your God-given gifts and use them in His service to build God's kingdom; i.e., teach a Sunday school class, mentor youth, volunteer in the church office, go on mission trips, serve in a soup kitchen, et cetera. Be a faithful steward of your time, talents and treasures.

WHY BECOME A "BORN AGAIN" CHRISTIAN AND FOLLOW JESUS?

- Gain Eternal life and the assurance of Heaven
  [Ecclesiastes 3:11, John 14:1-6, 1 John 5:11-12]

- Become a child of God and a joint heir with Jesus
  [Romans 8:17]

- Discover God's plan for your life, and its purpose
  [Jeremiah 29:11]

- Receive and experience the Gifts of the Spirit
  [Galatians 5:22]

- Be forgiven of your sins and purified from all
  unrighteousness *[1 John 1:9]*

- Become a new creation in Christ; Receive a new heart
  and humble spirit *[2 Corinthians 5:17]*

- Acquire wisdom and understanding for life
  [Proverbs 4:7, James 1:5]

- Become a Disciple equipped to share the Gospel
  [Mark 16:15]

- Develop a Biblical worldview. Renew your mind
  [Romans 12:2]

- Experience the Peace of God *[John 16:33]*

- To Love God and love your neighbor as yourself
  [Luke 10:27]

- To be able to flee from temptations *[1 Corinthians 10:13]*

- Not be deceived by Satan's lies, "Did God really say.......?"

- To know and claim the Bible's Promises for God's children
  [John 14:1-6, Matthew 11:28-30, John 11:26, Isaiah 40:31]

- Be able to contend for and defend the faith
  [Christian apologetics]

- Know 'His-Story' and God's plan for mankind
  [Genesis to Revelation]

- Live in obedience to God's rules for life, i.e., Ten
  Commandments, and enjoy His presence now and forever
  [Exodus 20:1-17]

- Learn from the great men and women, heroes of the
  Faith, recorded in the Bible *[Hebrews 11]*

- To have a life-transforming, personal intimate, and
  eternal relationship with Jesus Christ *[1 John 5:11-12]*

- To receive and enjoy the Glorious Riches that are in Jesus *[Philippians 4:19]*

  1. Redemption from sin

  2. Salvation and eternal life

  3. Wisdom and discernment

  4. Objective moral standards

  5. Peace, love, joy, kindness, patience, hope, goodness

  6. Grace, healing, mercy, and forgiveness

  7. Self-restraint, endurance, perseverance, character,

     And Much More!!!

SEEKERS AND SKEPTICS FAQS – BIBLICAL ANSWERS
QUESTIONS ABOUT GOD, JESUS, THE BIBLE AND CHRISTIANITY THAT YOU NEED TO BE ABLE TO ANSWER.

These questions are ones Disciple Makers will definitely encounter and ones which must be answered with both evidence and reason. The Apostle Paul is frequently quoted as "reasoning" with those to whom he is presenting the Gospel and providing evidence of Jesus resurrection and being the promised Messiah and the Son of God *[Acts 17:2, 18:9]*.

We have provided brief answers to those questions for your convenience. To get more details, we strongly recommend acquiring and reading a copy of both books referenced in the following note. Of course, you can also search for and find the answers in a good reference Bible like, The Life Application (NIV). We have tried to make it easier for you to find the answers with the noted pages in the two books.

NOTE: 'A' *is the book, "Answers to Your Greatest Questions" by Jack Dannemiller available at livingdialog.org.*
'T' is the book, "To Know With Certainty" by Lee Southard available at ToKnowWithCertainty.com. Both books are also available on Amazon.com and Christian Book Sellers.

- **How do I know that God exists?**
Evidence. Intelligent Design of the universe and all nature, i.e., DNA, and the intricate laws that govern the sciences. *T p.1, A p.11*

- **How do I know the Bible is God's Word?**
Prophecy. God knows the future as He exists outside of time and space. The Bible is a miracle as it was written over a period of 1,500 years by 40 authors and is in complete harmony with no contradictions. *T pp.21-24, A pp.125&153*

- **Was Jesus a real historical person?**
Evidence. The biblical and secular records, Josephus' and Tacitus' historical Chronicles of the period, confirm Jesus as an authentic historical person. *T p.7*

- **How can I know that Jesus was the promised Messiah?**
Prophecy. Jesus fulfilled over 100 prophetic pronouncements, many dating back 1,000 years before His birth, of His being the promised Messiah. *T p.9, A p.72*

- **Did Jesus really come back from the dead?**
Evidence. Jesus was seen by the 11 disciples at least three times and by over 500 other witnesses during His 40 days on the Earth after His resurrection prior to His ascension into heaven which was witnessed also by many. Jesus' resurrection became the foundation of the Christian faith and the good news of the gospel. *T p.15, A p.74*

- **Don't all religions offer a path to God and Heaven?**
No. Jesus stated himself that He is the only way to eternal life, peace with God and heaven *[John 14:6]*. The founders of all the other world religions are dead. They offered no hope for eternal life. *A p.155*

- **Is Christianity exclusively claiming Jesus is the only way to Heaven and eternal life?**
Yes. The Bible confirms it in many verses. *A p.71, [John 3:16, 1 John 5:11-12]*

- **How could a loving God condemn anyone to Hell?**
God does not. People reject his gracious offer of salvation in Jesus and choose to go there. A loving God wants all to have a relationship with him, but each person has a free will to decide. God honors the choices that they make. *A p.20*

- **Why would anyone want to follow Jesus?**
Benefits. Jesus alone offers meaning and purpose for life, answered prayers, eternal life and the gifts of the spirit: joy, love, peace, patience, kindness, goodness, faithfulness and so much more. *A p.78*

- **Isn't the Bible full of contradictions?**
No. There are different descriptions of a few events just like witnesses' observations of a crime or accident but no contradictions. So, when accounts of events are taken as a composite, a more complete description is provided. *T p.35, A p.130*

- **Why should I believe in Creation vs. Evolution?**
Evidence. The fossil record supports and confirms Creation. There has never been a single piece of transitional evidence to demonstrate one species becoming another, i.e., Evolution. There are mutations and variations within species but dogs are still dogs and horses are still horses. Science has now confirmed that there are at least 50 variables that must be perfectly

REASONS FOR THE FAITH

aligned for there to be any lifeforms whatsoever on planet Earth. This is called the Anthropic Principle. These discoveries affirm God's Intelligent Design providing even more evidence for the Christian faith and Creation. The probability of these factors existing from Evolution is zero. In fact, Evolution is a religion, no God, masquerading as a science, no evidence. *T p. 81-91, A p.43*

Answers to these questions offer sufficient reasons for and evidence of the validity of the claims of the Christian Faith.

After answering some or all of these questions, the other person has the choice to believe and accept Jesus as Savior or reject God's offer of salvation, God's Grace.

Remember, it is never a lack of reasons or evidence upon which a decision is made but of the person's heart and will to trust God's Word or go their own way at their own peril. A Disciple's role is to present the Gospel. The Holy Spirit saves!

INTRO TO JESUS' USE OF APOLOGETICS

By Geisler & Zuherin

Edited and adapted for Small Group Study By JCD

The historical use of apologetics, reasoned arguments and justification of something, someone or a cause, goes back to the time of the Greeks and Socrates. It became known as the Socratic Method, persuading with reason and evidence. Jesus used apologetics to establish His credentials as the prophesied Messiah, the Son of Man and the Son of God. As we might expect, Jesus is a 'Grand Master' of apologetics. He employed all of its techniques to make a case for Himself and His cause, i.e., to establish the Kingdom of God and bring redemption to a fallen and sinful world.

This brief look at the apologetics of Jesus which follows is included so that His disciples can learn from His example.

NOTE: More details can be found in the referenced book by Geisler and Zuherin.

1. Jesus' use of testimony - Witnesses to the events
   a. John the Baptist - "The lamb of God that takes away the sins of the world." *[John 1:29]*
   b. God the Father - "My beloved Son in whom I am well pleased." *[Mark 1:11, Matthew 3:17and 5:17]*
   c. Miracles, Works and Signs – "No one could perform the signs you are doing if God were not with him." *[John 3:2]*
   d. Scripture - Prophecies of the Messiah-Fulfill the Law, Prophets and Psalms *[Matthew 5:17]*
   e. Moses – Moses wrote the Law given by God, and Jesus
   f. The testimony of a sinless life; Jesus' perfect life demonstrates His testimony is true *[John 8:41, 46, 52]*.

Therefore, in making his case that he is the Messiah and the Son of God, Jesus gives reasons and evidence, i.e., apologetics – The use of testimony!

2. Jesus used miracles to verify His claim as the Son of God:
    a. Creation, human life, Mosaic period (Egypt) verified Moses was God's person.
    b. Prophets – God's messengers about God's acts of Divine judgment. *[John 10:24, 25, 38]*
    c. Apostles' Miracles

Jesus' miracles confirm his claim to be the Son of God and the authority over every realm of nature. He created everything including the laws that govern it but was not subject to them, i.e., walks on water, calms the storms, feeds the 5,000, raises the dead, etc. Remember, if God exists, miracles are possible, i.e., they are supernatural special acts of God. Acts that offer many infallible proofs of Jesus' claim.

3. Jesus' resurrection - A verifiable proven historical event – over 500 witnesses plus the 11 Apostles and the dramatic conversion of Paul, i.e., "resurrected to new Creation in Christ."

4. Jesus' use of reason — He used all the laws of logical reasoning. God said, "Come let us reason together." Jesus reasoned with the authorities and confounded them with his wisdom, which was far superior to theirs.

5. Jesus' use of parables -They taught valuable lessons and were memorable:
    a. The Good Samaritan
    b. The Prodigal Son
    c. Parables illustrate truth through stories. Jesus was the greatest storyteller that ever lived.

Remember His "I Am" statements:
    i.   Bread of life
    ii. Light of the world
    iii. Gate for the sheep
    iv. The Good Shepherd
    v. The Resurrection and the Life
    vi. The Way, the Truth and the Life
    vii. The True Vine
    viii. Prince of Peace

6. Jesus' use of prophecy – The fulfillment of Old Testament prophecies. Over 100 during his first coming.

7. Jesus' use of Arguments for God:
   a. Cosmological – First Cause, a beginning must have a beginner, God!
   b. Anthropological - Human beings made in the image of God are able to think and reason. Humans have an inner sense to worship. God has placed eternity in the hearts of mankind.
   c. Teleological - Nature itself and its incredibly Intelligent Design. Something only God could do.
   d. The Moral Argument - knowledge of good and evil, right and wrong – Conscience – The source of objective morality, God!

FINAL THOUGHTS: Even though Jesus was the greatest apologist of all time, He affirmed that no person can be brought to God without the ministry of the Holy Spirit. It is the Holy Spirit who convinces people of sin and the need for a Savior and brings about conversion.

Remember, it is never a lack of reasons for evidence upon which a decision is made, but one of a person's heart and will to trust God's word or go their own way at their own peril. A disciple's role is to present the Gospel. That's why Christian Apologetics is important. The Holy Spirit saves.

MY FRIEND POEM

This poem has purposely been placed near the end of your journey instead of on the last page as a reminder and motivator for you to be a faithful disciple of Jesus, who fearlessly and confidently shares the Gospel with friends, family, neighbors and colleagues.

MY FRIEND

By D. J. Higgins

My friend, I stand in judgment now
And feel that you're to blame somehow
While on this Earth I walked with you day by day
And never did you point the way

You knew the Lord in truth and glory
But never did you tell the story
My knowledge then was very dim
You could have led me safe to Him

Though we lived together here on Earth
You never told me of the second birth
And now I stand this day condemned
Because you failed to mention Him

You taught me many things, that's true
I call you friend and trusted you
But now I learned, now it's too late
You could have kept me from this fate

We walked by day and talked by night
And yet you showed me not the light
You let me live, love and die
All the while you knew I would never live on high

Yes, I called you friend in life
And trusted you in joy and strife
Yet in coming to this end
I see you really weren't my friend

Finally, several additional resources have been identified and suggested for your study, and tools provided so that you can become equipped with the soul-saving 'Words of Life' and with the essentials of the dialogue process necessary to accomplish the mission. The mission is to be about Jesus' Great Commission given for all believers as you are going in life.

In other words, tell everyone in your 'world' the Good News that the only way to heaven and eternal life is by faith in Jesus Christ *[Ephesians 2:8]*. I encourage you to make the statement found in *Romans 1:16*, "I will not be ashamed of the gospel of Christ for it is the power of God unto salvation for all who believe," your Motto.

When you obey Jesus' command, you can know for certain that one day when you are face-to-face with Jesus, you'll hear the best praise ever, "Well done, good and faithful servant, enter into the joy prepared for you before the foundation of the world." *[Matthew 25:34]*

See Appendix for additional Apologetics Resources.

AFTERWORD

This phase of your journey is complete. You have learned the mean-ing of the word, apologetics. You have read its definition relative to the Christian faith; What Christians believe, Why they believe it, and Why it's important to know and understand. You have been exposed to the topic of Dialogue and how to use it to share the gospel effectively and with confidence. You have been provided with suggested spiritual conversation 'openers' and some of the many questions you will encounter. You have been instructed on how to respond to those questions, in love, with Biblical answers. You have been equipped with reasons, facts, evidence, and truths to be able to both contend for and defend the faith.

In your "backpack" for the trail ahead are 'Gems of Wisdom,' resources you can draw on along the path as you are going about fulfilling the Great Commission of Jesus. It will be one of the most exciting and rewarding adventures in your life. You will be joined on the journey with Jesus and the Holy Spirit as your guides. Together you will build God's kingdom by leading friends, family, and others to a life-transforming relationship with Jesus.

Our team at Living Dialog Ministries considers it a privilege to be your resource partner in this journey. Enjoy the adventure! Have fun and Praise The Lord for the opportunities that lie ahead. May the Grace of our Lord Jesus Christ be with you. Amen!

APPENDIX - SUPPLEMENTAL RESOURCES & REFERENCES

- *NIV - Life Application Bible* - Zondervan

- *Evidence That Demands A Verdict: Life-Changing Truth For A Skeptical World* - Josh McDowell & Sean McDowell

- *Surprised By Faith: A Skeptic Discovers More To Life Than What We Can See, Touch, And Measure* - Don Bierle

- *The Case For Christ: A Journalist's Personal Investigation Of The Evidence For Jesus* - Lee Strobel

- *Know What You Believe* also *Know Why You Believe* - Paul Little

- *Mere Christianity* - CS Lewis

NOTE: *Book resources are available from Christian Booksellers, Christianbook.com, Amazon.com, BarnesandNoble.com, LivingDialog.org, and ToKnowWithCertainty.com.*

Pathway to Heaven & Eternal Life

"For all have sinned and broken God's Laws." (Romans 3:23)

"But God demonstrates His own love for us in this: while we were still sinners, Christ died for us." (Romans 5:8)

"The wages of sin is death." All die! [both physical and spiritual death] (Romans 6:23)

"Unless someone is born again, he cannot see the kingdom of God." (John 3:3)

"God so loved the world that He gave His only begotten son, Jesus, that whoever believes in him will not perish but have eternal life. (John 3:16)

Jesus said, "I am the way, the truth and the Life. No one comes to the Father except through me." (John 14:6)

"If you confess with your mouth that Jesus Christ is Lord, and believe in Your heart that God has raised him from the dead you will be Saved." (Romans 10:9&10)

"I stand at the door and knock. If anyone hears my voice and opens the door, (Your Heart) I will come in." (Revelation 3:20)

Salvation is by God's Grace alone, through Faith alone, in Christ alone! There is no other name by which one can be saved or gain eternal Life!

A Sinners Prayer of Confession

Lord Jesus, I confess I am a sinner In need of a savior. I admit I have Broken your commandments. Please forgive me.

I invite you now into my heart as my Savior and Lord of my life.

I commit to repent from my sinful ways and thoughts and follow you all the days of my life.

I believe in my heart that you died on the Cross to pay the penalty for my sins.

I believe that you are the resurrected Messiah, Son of God, and are now seated at God's right hand hearing and accepting me as a child of God!

I thank you Jesus for your Amazing Grace that saved a sinner like me!

Next Steps in Your Faith Journey

First, share this exciting news with family, Friends and everyone you encounter. Spread the Good News of Jesus Christ with those you meet.

Next, begin reading your Bible daily. Start with the Gospel of John to get a first hand account of the life of Jesus. Read a daily Devotional.

Then attend a Christ centered, Bible teaching church, join a Bible study and use you talents to serve God!

Living Dialog MINISTRIES

www.livingdialog.org

Source: Disciples Makers Toolbox Bookmark [Front]

Source: Disciples Makers Toolbox Bookmark [Back]

WHAT HAPPENS WHEN I DIE?
DISCOVER THE BIBLICAL ANSWER

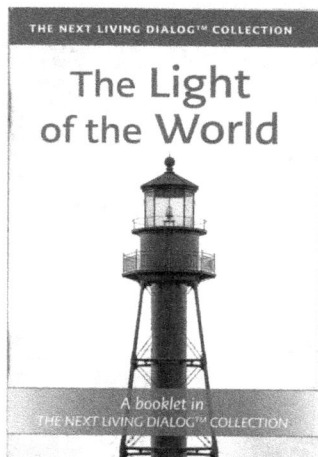

THE NEXT LIVING DIALOG™ COLLECTION

The Light of the World

A booklet in
THE NEXT LIVING DIALOG™ COLLECTION

What happens when I die? is a questions that has been mulled by the world's most renown philosophers and men and women from every walk of life, in every corner of the world, since people understood the concept of death.

In this 28-page booklet you will learn that God made you, along with all the rest of mankind, in His image. He desires a relationship with you just as all good fathers desire a relationship with their sons and daughters.

Packed with supporting scripture, *The Light of the World* will help you better understand God and his plan to reconcile sinful men and women to himself. Here you will find the answer to the question: *What happens when I die?*

The Light of the World is available from Living Dialog Ministries (TLDM). Order a copy for yourelf and another to share with a friend:

www.LivingDialog.org

Living Dialog ™
MINISTRIES

Be a new creation